ELDEN JOHNSON

The Prehistoric Peoples of Minnesota

Revised Third Edition

Minnesota Prehistoric Archaeology Series, No. 3

MINNESOTA HISTORICAL SOCIETY PRESS
ST. PAUL • 1988

2004 reprint of 1988 edition

♾™ The paper used in this publication meets the minimum
requirements of the American National Standard for
Information Sciences—Permanence for Printed Library
Materials, ANSI Z39.48-1984.

Minnesota Historical Society Press, St. Paul 55102

5 4 3 2
Manufactured in the United States of America

Library of Congress Cataloging-in-Publication Data

Johnson, Elden.
   The prehistoric peoples of Minnesota / by Elden Johnson.—Rev.
3rd ed.
      p. cm.—(Minnesota prehistoric archaeology series; no. 3)
      Bibliography: p.
      ISBN 0-87351-223-5 (pbk.)
      1. Indians of North America—Minnesota—Antiquities.
   2. Minnesota—Antiquities.   I. Title.   II. Series.
E78.M7J6 1988
977.6′00497—dc19   87-34663

International Standard Book Number: 0-87351-223-5

Contents

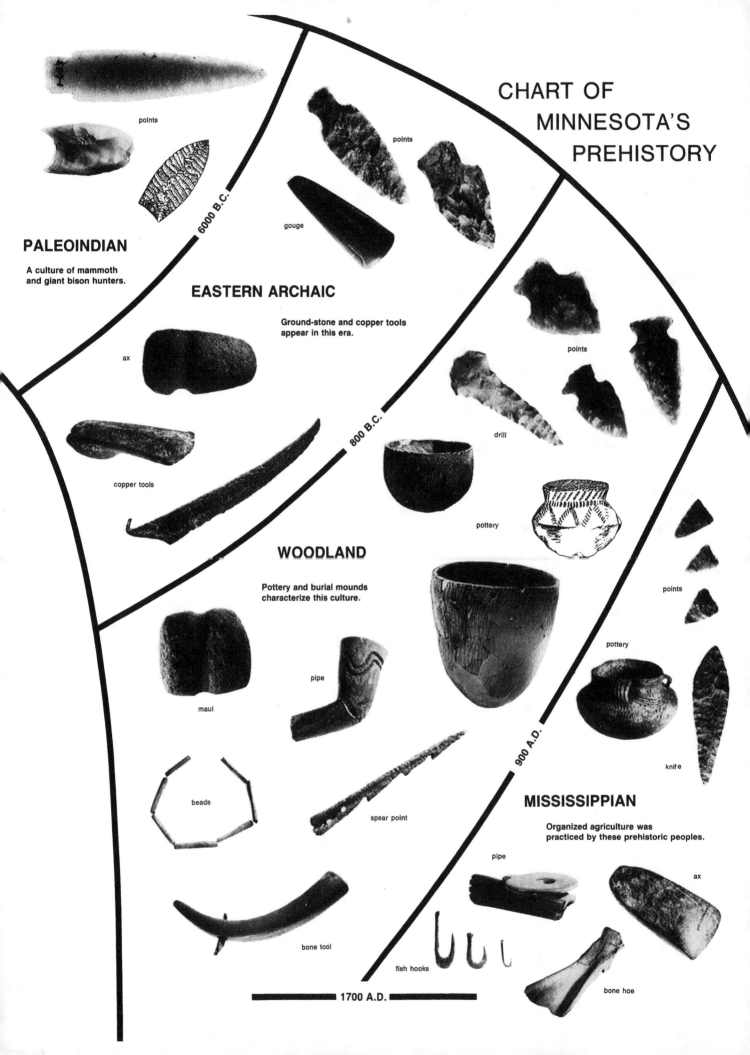

CHART OF MINNESOTA'S PREHISTORY

points

6000 B.C.

PALEOINDIAN

A culture of mammoth and giant bison hunters.

points

gouge

EASTERN ARCHAIC

Ground-stone and copper tools appear in this era.

ax

points

800 B.C.

drill

copper tools

pottery

WOODLAND

Pottery and burial mounds characterize this culture.

points

pottery

maul

pipe

knife

900 A.D.

beads

spear point

MISSISSIPPIAN

Organized agriculture was practiced by these prehistoric peoples.

pipe

ax

bone tool

fish hooks

bone hoe

1700 A.D.

Introduction

WHEN FRENCH EXPLORERS first reached what is now Minnesota in the seventeenth century, they found groups of native Americans living in every area of the state. In the south, village farmers planted gardens of maize or corn but depended on wild plant and animal foods of the prairies and forests for much of their diet. These southern groups, known later as the Iowa and Oto, were historic representatives of what archaeologists call the Mississippian cultural tradition. In central and western Minnesota lived the Dakota or Sioux. Those in east-central Minnesota, in the region of Mille Lacs and Big Sandy lakes, were the Santee or Eastern Dakota; those occupying the lands from Leech Lake south to the Minnesota River were the Yankton and Yanktonai Dakota; and on the western prairies were the Teton. The Assiniboin, close linguistic relatives of the Dakota, lived in the region from Lake of the Woods west to the Red River Valley; ancestral Cheyenne occupied the lower Red River Valley, and the Algonkin-speaking Cree were in the extreme northeast. The ancestors of today's Ojibway or Anishinabe peoples (also known as Chippewa) of northern Minnesota had not yet moved into the region from their central Great Lakes homeland. The central and northern Minnesota native American groups depended upon wild food resources for their sustenance (although some grew small amounts of tobacco and corn in favorable locations); they were the historic representatives of the Woodland archaeological tradition.

The ancestors of the native American groups encountered by the French visitors in the seventeenth century are Minnesota's prehistoric peoples. Prehistory is the earliest record of human life; it is differentiated from history as a convenience and as a reflection of the very different sources of information available. What we label history depends primarily on written records; what we call prehistory lacks written records and depends primarily on the record of human lives that is left in the earth. Archaeologists study the lives of the prehistoric peoples of Minnesota through the careful excavation and analysis of the archaeological record buried in the earth. What they have found and what they have learned about Minnesota's prehistory is the subject of this booklet.

All of Minnesota's native American groups descended from the peoples who left their homeland in northeastern Asia and became the first humans to enter North America. During later phases of the

Archaeologists excavating the Cooper Village Site in Mille Lacs-Kathio State Park. At right is a circular fire pit, which shows up as a dark area in the lighter subsoil.

Pleistocene Era (the age of the glaciers), a bridge of land connected extreme western Alaska and northeastern Asia. So much of the earth's water was locked on land in the form of glacial ice that the levels of the seas were lowered, and areas that are now water covered were exposed land surfaces. What is now the Bering Sea separating the Asian and North American continents was then a continuous land surface estimated to have been several hundred miles wide from north to south; it was covered with a northern tundra vegetation. Hunting peoples of the Pleistocene Era in northeastern Asia slowly moved into new, unpopulated territories where unexploited wild food resources allowed their growing populations to live successfully. During this process, probably extending over many thousands of years, the ancestors of the native Americans moved into North America. Their descendants filtered south over long periods of time until some had reached the southern tip of South America, where archaeological evidence shows that native Americans hunted and collected wild foods by 7000 B.C. These early peoples brought with them knowledge of the use of fire; tools and weapons of chipped stone, bone, antler, and wood; clothing made of animal skins; and an intimate knowledge of the behavior of the animals they hunted and the plant foods they gathered. They lived in small groups we call bands and moved about seasonally as the sources of food changed.

The date that these first arrivals reached North America is uncertain. Some anthropologists suggest that the earliest groups may have been in the New World 30,000 or more years ago. It is certain, however, that by 10,000 B.C. they had occupied most of the New World and had adapted their ways of life to widely divergent environments. In 10,000 B.C. in present-day New Mexico and on the western high Plains of North America, for example, a highly developed big game hunting culture had developed that is labeled by archaeologists the Llano Culture. It had two major components known as Clovis and Fol-

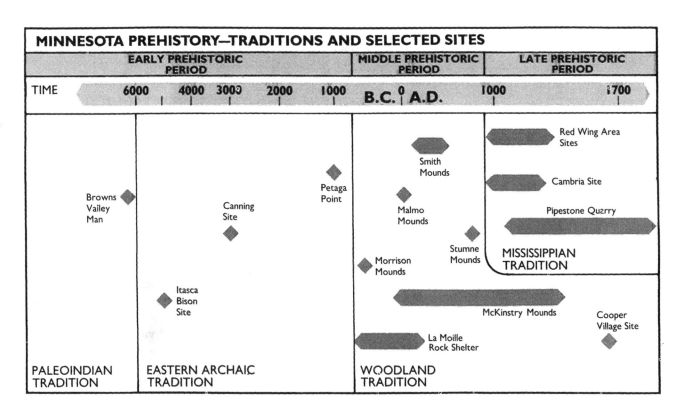

MINNESOTA PREHISTORY—TRADITIONS AND SELECTED SITES

| EARLY PREHISTORIC PERIOD | | MIDDLE PREHISTORIC PERIOD | LATE PREHISTORIC PERIOD |

TIME 6000 4000 3000 2000 1000 B.C. | A.D. 0 1000 1700

Browns Valley Man

Canning Site

Itasca Bison Site

Petaga Point

Smith Mounds

Malmo Mounds

Morrison Mounds

Stumne Mounds

La Moille Rock Shelter

McKinstry Mounds

Red Wing Area Sites

Cambria Site

Pipestone Quarry

MISSISSIPPIAN TRADITION

Cooper Village Site

PALEOINDIAN TRADITION

EASTERN ARCHAIC TRADITION

WOODLAND TRADITION

som, named for sites in New Mexico. It may be that descendants of these sophisticated hunters made up the first small groups to enter the Minnesota area as the lingering glacial ice melted and opened the landscape.

These first migrants into Minnesota encountered a very different climate and vegetation from that known to the historic native Americans. As the ice melted and the released water flowed to the rivers and newly formed lakes, a northern spruce forest covered the land surface. The early postglacial climate then changed rapidly and drastically. By 6000 B.C. temperatures rose to maximums much higher than we experience today, and a corresponding shift in vegetation occurred. The northern Plains grasslands expanded far to the east and for 3,000 to 4,000 years Minnesota was dominated by prairies. Pine and deciduous trees, such as maple, basswood, elm, and oak, replaced most of the remnant spruce forests in extreme northeastern Minnesota. Then, as the climate cooled slightly and precipitation increased at the end of the postglacial temperature maximum, a vegetation pattern developed more like that known historically.

The Minnesota prehistoric archaeological record is one of cultural changes that reflect the adaptation of lifeways to new conditions, and it is a record of differing modes of those adaptations to the varying environments that characterize the region. Archaeologists divide the eras of prehistoric time in Minnesota into Early, Middle, and Late Prehistoric periods. These are arbitrary divisions, and it is cultural changes seen in the archaeological record that mark the divisions between the periods. The Early Prehistoric Period ends and the Middle Prehistoric Period begins when the use of pottery and the burial of humans in earthen mounds appear in the archaeological record. Pottery and burial mounds represent a distinct cultural change, one that is perhaps more useful to archaeologists than to the populations of the time whose lifeways did not alter dramatically. The archaeological marker for the beginning of the Late Prehistoric Period is the appearance of the first maize-bean-squash farming in southern Minnesota—a change that does mean significant lifeway alterations beyond new food sources.

Archaeologists also define major cultural traditions that can be seen in the archaeological record. The earliest in Minnesota is a Paleoindian or Big Game Hunting tradition, like that of the early Clovis and Folsom hunters. As adaptive modes changed, Paleoindian descendants placed greater emphasis on the use of a wide variety of food resources, and a technological innovation in the manufacture of ground-stone (in addition to chipped-stone) tools appears to mark the beginning of the Eastern Archaic tradition. The Woodland tradition is that which begins with the addition of pottery and burial mounds to an Eastern Archaic tradition lifeway, and the Mississippian tradition is marked by the first farmers.

Within traditions archaeologists define specific cultures (like the Laurel Culture described later), with each culture comprising a series of related archaeological sites. The latter are geographically located places, identifiable archaeologically, where activities took place among peoples sharing a common cultural tradition. A site may thus have been a village, a hunting camp, a garden area, a burial place, a canoe portage, or any other location where people met for a purpose and left a record of their activities in the earth.

Minnesota has many thousands of archaeological sites, but only a few thousand have been identified and their locations recorded, and even fewer have been excavated by archaeologists. The "data bank" or collected information we have today is only a sample of the record of prehistoric peoples in Minnesota. As towns and cities grow, as lakeshores continue to be developed, and as modern alteration of the landscape of Minnesota accelerates, the archaeological record continues to diminish. Thus there is an urgent need for the protection and investigation of undisturbed archaeological sites in Minnesota. Knowledge of the cultural heritage of native Americans is important to all of us, and the record of human history in Minnesota is an important part of the history of humans on this earth.

In this third edition of *The Prehistoric Peoples of Minnesota* many changes have been made that reflect the acceleration of archaeological research in Minnesota since the first edition appeared in 1969 and the second edition was published in 1978. Knowledge of past human behavior and cultural systems is never static; it grows and changes as archaeological investigations continue, as new analytic methods develop, and as new insights into the interpretation of the past are shared. This edition attempts to incorporate some of this new knowledge.

All objects illustrated in this booklet are from the site collections of the University of Minnesota unless otherwise designated. Usually they have not been photographed to actual size or drawn to scale. A large number of the items were photographed by Alan Ominsky, who also designed this booklet. Other photographs on the following pages are also from the University of Minnesota unless credited to a different source.

Paleoindian Tradition

THE ARCHAEOLOGICAL EVIDENCE supporting the presence in Minnesota of the earliest Paleoindian tradition peoples is disappointingly meager. There are no excavated archaeological materials that can definitely be attributed to the makers of either Clovis (sometimes called Eastern Fluted) or Folsom projectile points in Minnesota. There have been rare occurences or "finds" of isolated Clovis and Folsom projectile points on the surface of agricultural fields after plowing, and although there have been a number of finds of woolly mammoth skeletal parts and teeth at Minnesota localities, none has ever been indisputably associated with human activity. Similarly, Folsom points collected in Minnesota lack any association with the large prehistoric bison, as such finds have elsewhere in the United States. Spear points of these early forms have been found only in southern and southwestern Minnesota, suggesting that there were no populations in east-central or northern Minnesota during the Early Prehistoric Period. Intensive archaeological surveys of the shoreline areas of Glacial Lake Agassiz, the huge lake of glacial meltwater that once covered what is now the Red River Valley, located fluted spear points of both Clovis and Folsom types; they were found west of the Red River Valley in eastern North Dakota and northeastern South Dakota, but not in Minnesota on the eastern side of the glacial lake. It is only in the later phases of the Paleoindian tradition that archaeological evidence is accumulating to show human populations spreading throughout the state.

The finds relating to later peoples of this tradition, who were probably also bison hunters, include two types of beautifully chipped projectile points known as the Browns Valley and the Eden-Scottsbluff. The first of these takes its name from the Browns Valley site in western Minnesota accidentally discovered in October 1933 by William H. Jensen, an amateur archaeologist. He found the points in

The projectile point at the top of the page is an Eden-Scottsbluff point.

Clovis fluted projectile point and two Folsom points. Both types have been found in Minnesota.

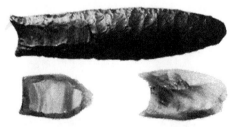

association with the human skeleton of an adult male buried in a pit dug into gravel at the outlet of Glacial Lake Agassiz. Knives of brown chalcedony also accompanied the burial.

Jensen observed fragments of human bones and a flaked point in a load of gravel brought to his grain elevator from the Browns Valley municipal gravel pit. He went immediately to the pit where he found other bone fragments and points. Recognizing their importance, he reported the discovery to Professor Albert E. Jenks at the University of Minnesota, who reexamined the site and recovered additional fragments and artifacts.

Geological evidence suggests that the burial was placed in the gravel ridge after the termination of the southern Glacial Lake Agassiz drainage but before there had been any appreciable soil formation on the gravel surface. No firm date can be assigned to the find known as Browns Valley Man, but similar projectile points uncovered at a Wyoming site date to almost 8,000 years ago. On the basis of presently available evidence, it seems likely that the Browns Valley burial dates from about 6000 B.C.

A second very old human skeleton—that of a teen-age female—was also found accidentally in the 1930s near Pelican Rapids in western Minnesota. First called Minnesota Man, its name was officially changed to Minnesota Woman in 1968. This find presented problems that archaeologists have not been able to solve satisfactorily.

On June 16, 1931, a highway maintenance crew working on a road that crossed the bed of an extinct body of water known as Glacial Lake Pelican exposed a shiny object some ten feet below the ground level. It proved to be a white shell. The workers did some further digging by hand and soon unearthed a human skull, which had been partially crushed. They also retrieved a broken tool made from an elk antler and a shell pendant of special interest because the shell came from salt water, probably the Gulf of Mexico. The men notified Professor Jenks, but by the time he reached the site the damage had been done: the skull had been removed, and it was too late for him to see the find in place in the earth. He later redug the site, however, and recovered more than three hundred additional bone fragments from the deposits of the glacial lake bed.

Browns Valley knife (top) and projectile point found in 1933 in association with the Browns Valley Man skeleton.

Prehistoric bison skull (below, left) in the collections of the Science Museum of Minnesota and teeth of the now extinct mammoth. Courtesy Science Museum of Minnesota.

Arguments have swirled about the Pelican Rapids find ever since its discovery. Most of the debate is over whether the skeleton is as old as the glacial deposits it was buried in or whether the girl lost her life later. Geologists date the lake bed clays to the late Pleistocene period, something less than 11,000 years ago. Estimates of the age of the skeleton have ranged all the way from 25,000 years to as late as the modern Dakota Indians of the historic period. If the find were as ancient as the glacial deposits in which it was buried, it might be North America's oldest known human skeleton, but the age question has not been resolved. We do not know whether this find belongs to the Paleoindian tradition or whether it should be placed in the later Eastern Archaic or Woodland traditions.

Later attempts at radiocarbon dating of the skeleton were inconclusive for several reasons—the residue carbon tested fell below the minimum amount required for accuracy in testing, and the skeleton had once been treated with shellac that contaminated the carbon present. While unsatisfactory and questionable, the radiocarbon date produced falls within the time allotted to the Eastern Archaic tradition, 6000 B.C. to 800 B.C. The extreme depth at which the skeleton was found below the surface would tend to support those who argue for an earlier age, since Indian burials are seldom deeply interred in the soil. It is the author's opinion that the radiocarbon date is probably correct, and the skeleton is of the Eastern Archaic tradition. The marine-shell pendant

William Jensen points to the discovery site in 1933 of the skeleton known as Browns Valley Man. Photo from American Anthropological Association, Memoirs No. 49 (1937).

MINNESOTA

Area Shown

This map shows the discovery sites of two early human skeletons near Browns Valley and Pelican Rapids.

Three projectile points of the Plano type dating from the Paleoindian tradition.

is shaky evidence for assigning a date, but such shells were rather widely distributed in the Archaic tradition, and they are not known from other sites of the Paleoindian tradition.

The site of this early find on U.S. Highway 59 just north of Pelican Rapids has been marked by the Minnesota Historical Society.

The final phases of the Paleoindian tradition are marked by varieties of beautifully flaked projectile points that are called Plano points. These are much more common in Minnesota's archaeological record and have been found throughout the state. One of the largest collections of Plano points is from the Reservoir Lakes region northwest of Duluth where Elaine Redepenning, an amateur archaeologist, has found such materials over a number of years. The Reservoir Lakes are impounded waters whose levels are drawn down seasonally. When the reservoirs are full, the action of waves erodes the banks, and when the water levels are down, Plano tools and flakes appear along the shoreline and at the edges of former islands. Redepenning not only collects these materials, but she also carefully maps the location of each find, numbers each artifact so that its "find spot" is keyed to the map, and keeps written records of her finds. She shares her work with archaeologists, who have been able to define a Reservoir Lakes Phase of the Paleoindian tradition and to publish this important record in the scientific literature.

It seems probable that the makers of the Reservoir Lakes points wintered in the forested areas just beyond the easternmost extension of the prairies during the period of the postglacial temperature maximum. If this is true, it would establish a system of exploiting the food resources of both grasslands and forests that characterizes the economic systems of many of the prehistoric peoples of the state throughout the succeeding periods.

Eastern Archaic Tradition

THE NEXT OLDEST TRADITION—the Eastern Archaic—differs from the earlier Paleoindian in both its tools and its foods. Here we can see the beginning of regional cultural variations, reflecting a greater exploitation of local environments in the use of different raw materials for food and tools. At some time during the period the Eastern Archaic peoples developed techniques for making ground- and pecked-stone implements in addition to the chipped-stone tools of the previous era. They also began to fashion woodworking tools such as axes and gouges, using basalt and granite as raw materials, and to make tools of copper, which indicates a change in technology.

Hunting of both large and small game animals formed one of the major pursuits of the Eastern Archaic peoples, who still followed a seminomadic way of life, shifting their small camps seasonally to utilize different food resources in various localities. The chipped-stone projectile points used for hunting developed a different form; they were now stemmed and notched and not as well made as those of the Paleoindian tradition. Chipped-stone scrapers, knives, punches, and drills were still made. The spear and dart continued, and fish—taken with a spear through the ice or in shallow water during spring spawning runs—served as a source of food. The presence of roasting pits for acorns and of wild cherry and plum pits in camp refuse sites also attests to the importance of wild plant foods among these peoples.

The earliest carefully reported site of the Eastern Archaic tradition is the Itasca Bison Kill Site in Itasca State Park. Here archaeologist C. Thomas Shay excavated into the deep peat layers of the Nicollet Creek Valley. Beneath the peat and on the surface of an underlying basal layer of lake-bed marl, laid down when the valley was an open-

The Old Copper projectile point above is in the Minnesota Historical Society collections.

A polished-stone gouge used for woodworking (below) and a grooved-stone ax from the Eastern Archaic tradition (right).

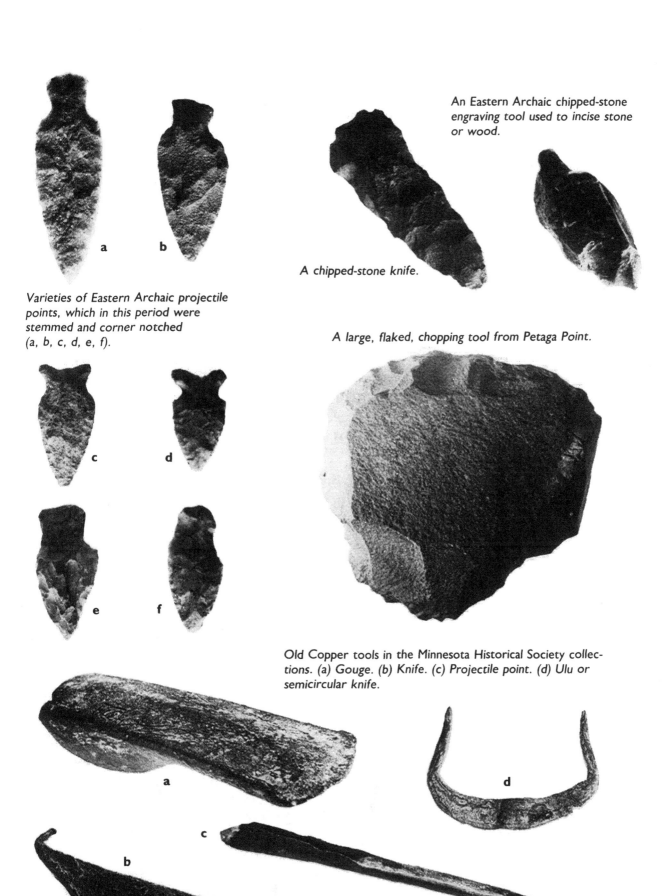

An Eastern Archaic chipped-stone engraving tool used to incise stone or wood.

A chipped-stone knife.

Varieties of Eastern Archaic projectile points, which in this period were stemmed and corner notched (a, b, c, d, e, f).

A large, flaked, chopping tool from Petaga Point.

Old Copper tools in the Minnesota Historical Society collections. (a) Gouge. (b) Knife. (c) Projectile point. (d) Ulu or semicircular knife.

water arm of Lake Itasca, he found bones of an early form of bison called *Bison occidentalis.* Some of the bones had been scratched and cut when the bison were butchered. With the bones Shay found occasional chipped-stone cutting and scraping tools that had been used in the butchering process. Radiocarbon dates indicate that between 7000 and 5000 B.C. the site was used by small groups of hunters who killed the bison as the animals forded the open lake arm at the narrowest part of the valley. Analysis of the plant pollen preserved in the peat allowed Shay to reconstruct the vegetation that existed at the time the bison were hunted. Unlike the park today, where beautiful pine trees dominate the scene, the landscape around the bison kill site was dominated by prairie grasses interspersed with scattered oak trees—a vegetation pattern called an oak savannah. An interesting "first" at the Itasca site is the skeleton of a domestic dog, the earliest evidence we have for the presence of this animal in Minnesota.

A slightly later Eastern Archaic bison-processing camp, the Canning Site, lies in the Red River Valley floodplain in Norman County. Here Michael Michlovic, archaeologist at Moorhead State University, found a deeply buried and well-preserved campsite used between 4000 and 3000 B.C. Limb fragments are the most common segments of the bison skeleton found at the site, indicating that the bison were killed and partially butchered elsewhere, and then parts of the dismembered carcasses were brought to this camp for further processing. It is probable that the flesh was removed, cut into strips, and sun dried for preservation. Many chipped-stone hide scrapers were found at this site, suggesting that the hides of the bison were probably also treated.

Finds of copper tools used late in this period have occurred throughout the state, but they are most numerous in the east-central and northeastern areas. The use of native copper in Minnesota for tools and perhaps ritual objects is a part of a distinctive complex usual-

A bison skull, dating from the Eastern Archaic tradition, was found buried in a peat deposit at the Itasca bison site on Nicollet Creek in Itasca State Park at the headwaters of the Mississippi.

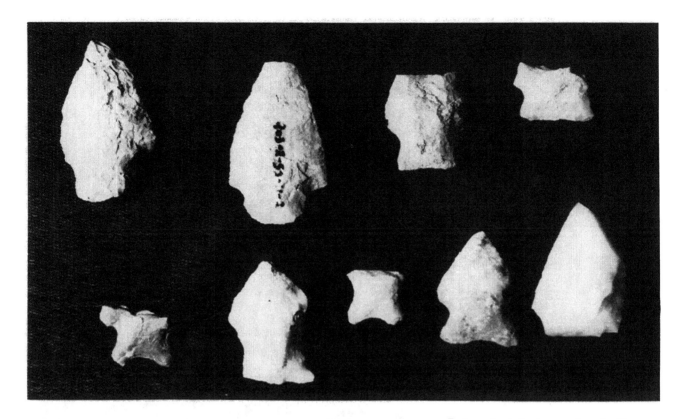

Eastern Archaic stemmed projectile points found at the Canning Site, a bison-processing camp in Norman County. Photo courtesy of Michael Michlovic, Moorhead State University.

ly called the Old Copper Complex, unique to the western Great Lakes region of Minnesota, Wisconsin, Upper Michigan, and parts of Manitoba and Ontario. Accidental finds of isolated copper implements are common throughout Minnesota, but their greatest concentration is in Wisconsin where a number of Old Copper human burial sites have been excavated. Perhaps beginning as early as 5000 B.C., the Old Copper Complex persisted until nearly 1000 B.C., and it provides the earliest evidence of the use of metals for tools in the New World. Copper was not sufficiently plentiful, however, to answer all of the needs of these Eastern Archaic peoples, who also continued to make and use stone tools. Copper continued to be used in the succeeding Middle and Late Prehistoric periods, but primarily as ornaments, and the distinctive, large, utilitarian copper tools of the Eastern Archaic disappear. Large-socketed and rattail-tanged spear points, small cone-shaped points, knives, fish gorges, and awls were made by hammering raw native copper into the desired shape. Copper-tool manufacture in this period was not a true metallurgical process, but it involved pounding and annealing nearly pure nuggets. This process necessitated locating pure raw copper that needed no smelting and refining. Such sources have long been known in the Upper Michigan peninsula, on Isle Royale in Lake Superior, and in glacial deposits where copper nuggets sometimes occur in the gravels transported by the glaciers from regions farther north. A Minnesota source appears to lie in the basalt outcrops near the Upper St. Croix River.

The first Old Copper habitation site to be excavated in Minnesota was worked by Peter Bleed in 1966. Known as Petaga Point, it is located on what is now the picnic ground in Mille Lacs-Kathio State Park. The site was investigated before park development took place, and Bleed's final report on its archaeology was published by the Minnesota Historical Society. The earliest evidences of human activity at Petaga Point belong to the Old Copper Culture. Tools excavated there appear

Aerial view of Petaga Point in Mille Lacs-Kathio State Park. The Rum River is at lower left.

to be late Eastern Archaic, and the copper projectile-point forms are dominated by the small cone-shaped point. Bleed suggested that the sources of copper used by the Petaga Point people may have been local in origin, perhaps the small deposits in the outcrops along the Snake and Kettle rivers that flow into the St. Croix.

While only a few Eastern Archaic sites have been investigated in Minnesota, surface finds are common throughout the state, and additional sites representing this tradition must be presumed to exist. Evidence found elsewhere suggests that Eastern Archaic populations remained small, but known sites in other states indicate the presence of greater numbers of people than existed in the earliest prehistoric period. Future archaeological work will undoubtedly enhance our present knowledge of this tradition in Minnesota.

Woodland Tradition

THE WOODLAND TRADITION, characterized by the presence of pottery vessels and burial mounds, begins in Minnesota somewhere between 1000 and 500 B.C. Its appearance marks the beginning of the Middle Prehistoric Period, during which the regional differences in culture that began in the Eastern Archaic become stronger. While populations may have grown slightly during this period, the basic economic system—dependent on fishing, collecting wild plant foods, using invertebrates such as clams, hunting a wide variety of both large and small mammals, and seasonal moving by small bands to exploit the natural foods of their region—remained much as it was during the Eastern Archaic tradition. The appearance of pottery and the construc-

The pottery vessel above is from the Blackduck Culture.

The round area shows the excavated clay lining of a wild rice threshing pit from the Woodland tradition.

tion of earthen mounds elaborate the cultures of this tradition but do not revolutionize them.

The tools and implements of Woodland peoples during this Middle Prehistoric Period are much like those of the preceding Eastern Archaic cultures. Projectile points vary more in form, and the stemmed point becomes rare, with side- and corner-notched points of several varieties supplanting it. Copper continues to be used for awls or piercing tools and ornaments, although the frequency of copper articles lessens. Scrapers, knives, drills, awls, and punches of chipped stone persist without great modification, and the ground-stone woodworking implements continue. The most common of the ground-stone tools is the grooved maul—a spherical stone, usually granite, about the size of a softball, encircled by a shallow groove and hafted on a wooden handle, probably using rawhide. These pounding tools were undoubtedly multipurpose, but they probably were commonly used to pound dried meat and berries. Their higher frequency in prairie-zone sites, where bison was a staple food, indicates this food preparation use.

Bone and antler tools and ornaments are found in many Woodland sites. They include hide scrapers, hide fleshers, awls and punches, carved dice for games, whistles made of bird bone, and barbed points for spearing muskrats and fish. Carved pendants of bone and shell are also found, as are necklaces that incorporate animal teeth and claws.

Tooth-edged projectile point (left) found in the Hoffman Mound near Alexandria. At right are various types of Woodland projectile points of chipped stone.

Among the earliest Woodland sites in Minnesota are the La Moille Rock Shelter near Winona, which was excavated by Professor Lloyd A. Wilford of the University of Minnesota in the late 1930s, and the Schilling Site on the tip of Grey Cloud Island in the Mississippi River bottoms near Hastings. These are habitation sites or campsites that have the earliest pottery known in Minnesota. The heavy-walled clay vessels are flower-pot shaped and have an exterior surface marked by impressions of twisted cordage. There is no other decoration on the vessels, nor is there any means of suspending them over a fire. They were used for cooking simply by placing the vessels in hot coals.

While it is not known exactly how the prehistoric Indians happened to devise the custom of building mounds, there is no doubt about the purpose they served; they were graves. Artificially erected heaps of earth are distributed over a wide area of the central United States. It has been estimated that Minnesota once had some 10,000 burial mounds scattered throughout the state. Many of them have now disappeared because of farming, road building, and general pub-

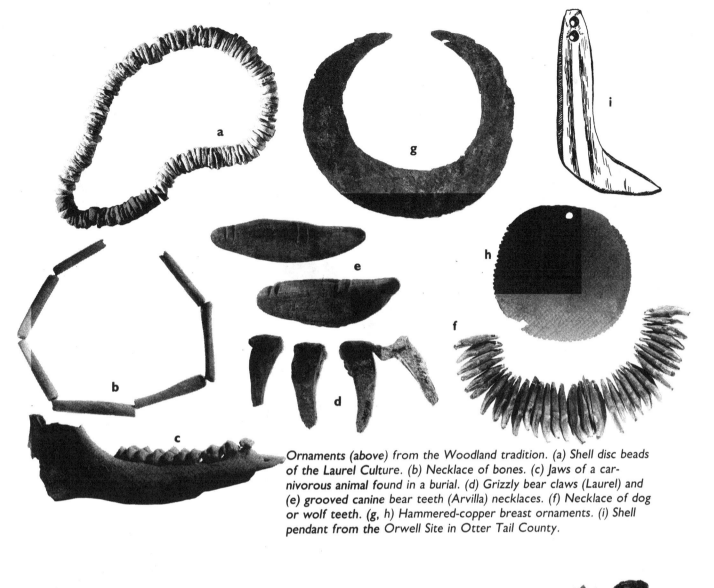

Ornaments (above) from the Woodland tradition. (a) Shell disc beads of the Laurel Culture. (b) Necklace of bones. (c) Jaws of a carnivorous animal found in a burial. (d) Grizzly bear claws (Laurel) and (e) grooved canine bear teeth (Arvilla) necklaces. (f) Necklace of dog or wolf teeth. (g, h) Hammered-copper breast ornaments. (i) Shell pendant from the Orwell Site in Otter Tail County.

Below are ground-stone tools of the Woodland tradition. (a) Milling stone. (b) Tube probably used by a shaman to suck illness from the body (Blackduck Culture). (c) Grooved maul, the most common stone tool of this period.

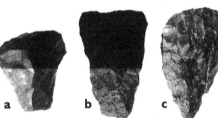

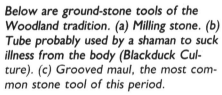

Various chipped-stone tools of the Woodland tradition. Above are three hide scrapers (a-c), a side scraper (d), and a punch (e). Below are stone drills (f, g), an engraving tool (h), and two knives (i, j).

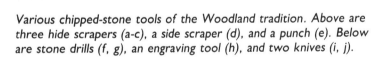

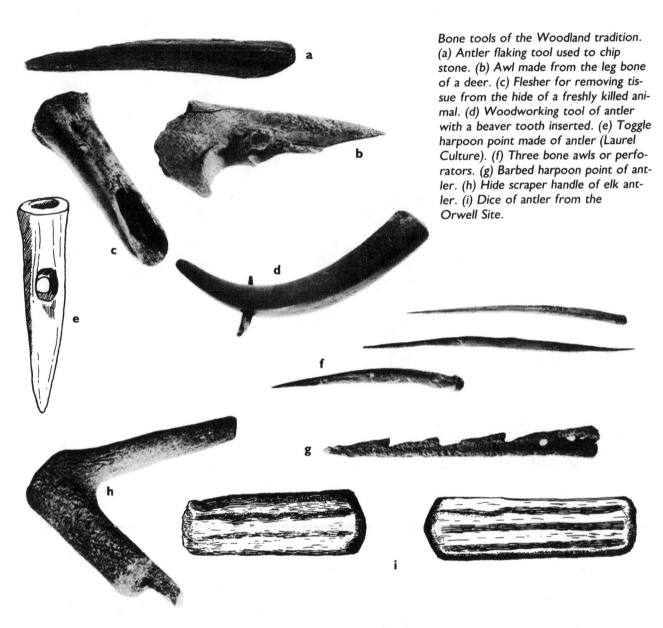

Bone tools of the Woodland tradition. (a) Antler flaking tool used to chip stone. (b) Awl made from the leg bone of a deer. (c) Flesher for removing tissue from the hide of a freshly killed animal. (d) Woodworking tool of antler with a beaver tooth inserted. (e) Toggle harpoon point made of antler (Laurel Culture). (f) Three bone awls or perforators. (g) Barbed harpoon point of antler. (h) Hide scraper handle of elk antler. (i) Dice of antler from the Orwell Site.

Excavating a habitation area of the Smith Site, near the Grand Mound. The Rainy River is in the background.

lic carelessness. The burial-mound concept was elaborated as the Woodland cultures grew, and in central and northern Minnesota, burial in mounds persisted until the arrival of Europeans.

The mounds took several forms. The most numerous of those remaining are circular and dome-shaped or conical. Most are quite small—about 35 feet in diameter and less than two feet in height. Some, however, are very large. These were built in several stages by adding successive layers of earth over the years.

Long, linear mounds that resemble railway embankments are found in central Minnesota, and a very few effigy mounds in the shape of birds or animals once existed along the Wisconsin border from the Twin Cities southward. All of the latter have disappeared. An interesting group containing both linear and circular mounds can be seen in Tamarac National Wildlife Refuge near Detroit Lakes in Becker County. The Stumne Mounds on the Snake River near Pine City are an excellent example of an undisturbed linear mound group, which is being preserved as a state prehistoric site.

Most of the Minnesota mounds that have been excavated contain what archaeologists call "primary" and "secondary" burials, although both types do not usually occur in the same mound. In a primary burial, the entire body is interred, usually in subsoil pits below the mound. The body is typically in an upright, flexed position with the knees drawn up and the head resting on them. Burials of this type frequently have grave goods that include both tools and ornaments.

A secondary burial consists of the partial remains of a body that was first placed in the open on a platform or tied in a tree, or a body that was originally buried in a shallow pit and later exhumed. These small secondary "bundle burials," as they are called, are the most numerous in excavated Minnesota mounds. Usually they consist of the bones of the arms and legs, the skull, and sometimes the lower jaw. Only rarely do grave goods accompany secondary bundle burials. The earliest

Aerial view of the Stumne Mounds near Pine City. These linear burial mounds are owned by the state of Minnesota.

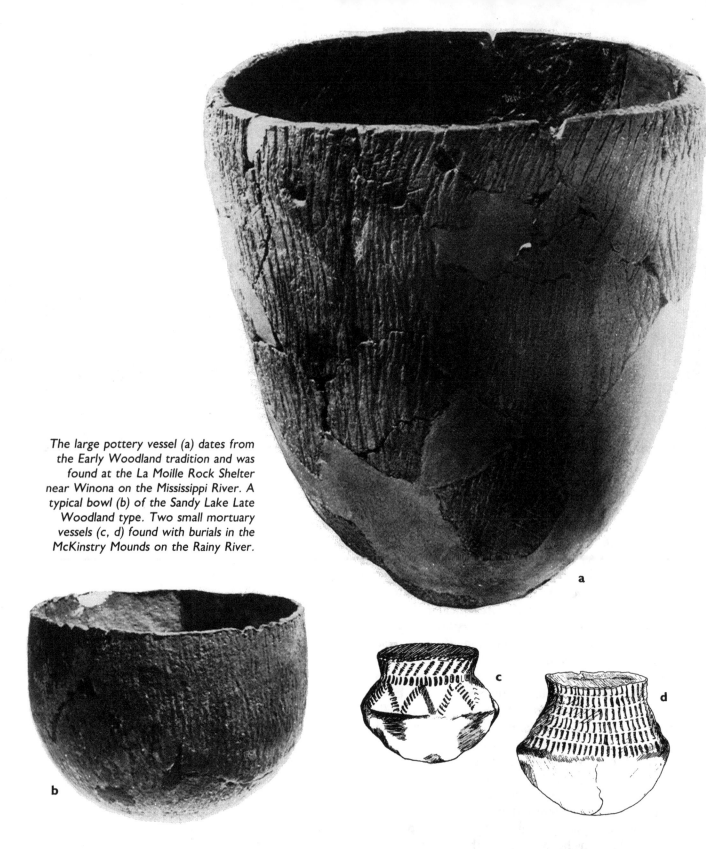

The large pottery vessel (a) dates from the Early Woodland tradition and was found at the La Moille Rock Shelter near Winona on the Mississippi River. A typical bowl (b) of the Sandy Lake Late Woodland type. Two small mortuary vessels (c, d) found with burials in the McKinstry Mounds on the Rainy River.

burial mound, radiocarbon dated at about 600 to 700 B.C., is one in the Morrison Mound Site located close to the outlet of Otter Tail Lake near Fergus Falls. That small, low, circular mound had a single, shallow, subsoil pit under its center. The pit had been covered with a layer of small logs overlying a single human burial, and a fire, probably ceremonial, at the edge of the burial pit had partially charred the logs. Over this was placed the earth that formed the mound. The burial itself was a secondary bundle burial. This form of mound and burial also

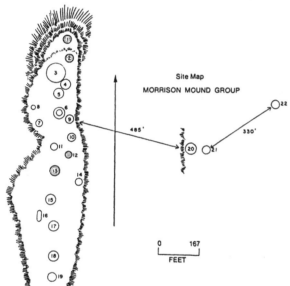

Site Map

MORRISON MOUND GROUP

485'

330'

0   167

FEET

The Morrison Mound group (above) at
the outlet of Otter Tail Lake in central
Minnesota is the earliest dated Woodland site in the state—690 B.C. The
mounds are being preserved by the Minnesota Historical Society. At left is a
map of the Morrison Mounds.

occurs at the Anderson Site near Mille Lacs Lake and in a mound near
Henderson in Sibley County; it is also common in northeastern Iowa.

The Grand Mound on the Rainy River at the state's northern border
is over 100 feet in diameter and more than 40 feet high. It is the largest
remaining prehistoric burial mound in the Upper Mississippi region.
The Grand Mound has not been excavated, although parts of it have
been badly disturbed by indiscriminate digging early in this century.
It and the other mounds that make up the Smith Site are now
preserved, and they are interpreted in the Grand Mound Interpretive
Center operated by the Minnesota Historical Society.

Cultural variation that reflects adaptation to very different environments leading to regional cultures during this period becomes clear in
a comparison of the Fox Lake sites of the southwestern prairie zone,
the Laurel sites of the far north, and the Malmo and Howard Lake sites
of the mixed forest zones of the east-central region. Fox Lake sites are
commonly located on the islands or peninsulas of prairie lakes.
Sheltered from the winds of the open prairies by the lakeshore and island trees, the peoples of these sites depended upon bison and a number of small lacustrine animals such as muskrat and beaver and upland
animals like deer, raccoon, and elk for their protein food sources; they

undoubtedly also ate plums, chokecherries, prairie turnips, and other vegetable foods of the region. Their pottery decoration is distinctive and consists of sharply incised lines traced around the exterior of the vessel rims in patterns of horizontal banding, crosshatching, and diagonal incisions. The floor of a small house, representing a winter dwelling, has been excavated by archaeologists from the Science Museum of Minnesota, and undoubtedly other similar structures await excavation at sites at Mountain Lake, Fox Lake, Lake Benton, and Fury Island, a county park near Worthington.

The northern Laurel sites have been studied more extensively than the others, and the Smith Site contains, in addition to the burial mounds, deeply stratified occupational remnants of Laurel peoples and of the succeeding Late Prehistoric Blackduck peoples. Laurel sites also are found on Lake Vermilion, on Nett Lake, in Voyageurs National Park, in the Red River Valley near Hallock, and across the Rainy River in Ontario. The food refuse from the westerly Laurel sites contains remains of moose and bison, indicating that Laurel populations utilized both the northern forested region and the prairies immediately west of Lake of the Woods. Sites on the Rainy River below International Falls contain quantities of the exterior boney plates of sturgeon; these huge fish were probably taken during the annual spring spawning season as they moved out of Lake of the Woods into the river.

Laurel pottery is also distinctive. It is thin-walled, fired to a very hard consistency, smooth surfaced, and decorated with impressions

Burial mound sites are not evenly distributed over the Minnesota landscape. One of the largest concentrations is in the Red Wing area near Prairie Island.

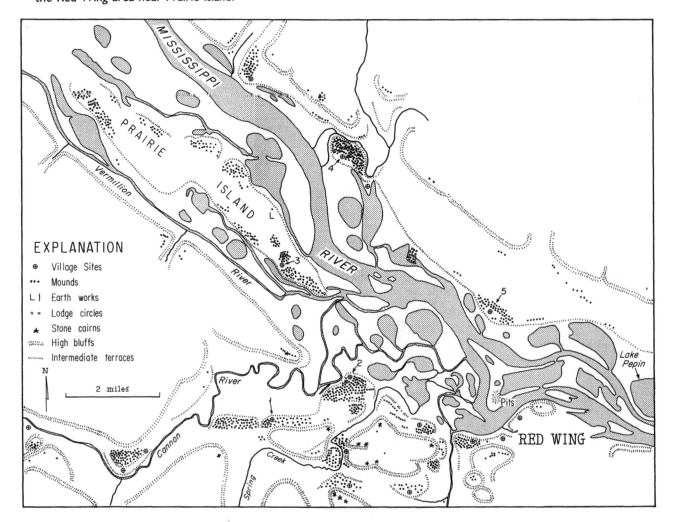

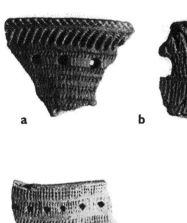

Decorated pottery rim sherds of Woodland cultures. (a, b) Blackduck designs using twisted cordage to impress the soft clay. (c,d) Laurel designs using dentate- or toothed-stamp impressions. Howard Lake-Malmo designs with (e) raised nodes and carved-stamp impressions and (f) impressions made with the end of a hollow reed.

made with a comblike instrument that archaeologists call a dentate stamp. Variations in the form of the dentate stamp and variations in the manner by which the stamp is impressed produce distinctive decorative modes.

The Malmo sites on Mille Lacs Lake and sites of a related culture called Howard Lake near the Twin Cities exhibit pottery decorative modes and patterns more like those of the Hopewellian cultures located in Illinois, southwestern Wisconsin, and northeastern Iowa. Dentate stamping is present, but more commonly fingernail impressions, circular impressions made with the end of a hollow reed stem, and repeated decorative units encircling the upper parts of the vessel are outlined with incised or drawn lines.

Like the populations of Laurel and Fox Lake cultures, those of the Malmo and Howard Lake cultural groups were small; their economic system was based on the use of a variety of foods seasonally, and they occupied fairly large territories over which they moved during the year as food resources became available. All buried their dead in earthen mounds, although the particular interment styles differed, as did mound construction practices. Malmo mounds, for example, are circular, dome-shaped, and usually represent one construction phase; these mound sites normally contain numerous small mounds representing a series of construction phases and a number of years. Laurel mounds, in contrast, while circular and dome-shaped, are cumulative mounds. Instead of constructing a new mound for additional burials in succeeding years, the Laurel peoples placed their burials on or in the upper surfaces of an existing mound and then added another layer of earth, increasing the height of the original mound. This is the way the Grand Mound, for example, reached its impressive size.

The Woodland tradition ends with the introduction of corn farming and the distinctive Mississippian cultures into southern Minnesota about 900 A.D. The Woodland cultures persist in central and northern Minnesota where short growing seasons prohibit effective corn farming, but they persist with significant cultural changes and with measurable population increases.

Several varieties of stone and pottery pipes of the Woodland tradition from Minnesota sites. Tobacco may have been traded into Minnesota from the south.

Mississippian Tradition

A NEW TRADITION, born in the southern United States and exhibiting strong Mexican influences, made itself felt in Minnesota during the Late Prehistoric Period. Mexican influences may be clearly seen in the southeastern United States, where pyramids were constructed. Principally, however, they appear in an intensification of the agricultural base and in the increasing size and complexity of the societies.

The Mississippian tradition entered Minnesota from two directions. The earliest intrusion, which was short-lived, appeared in the extreme southwestern portion of the state, entering from the Missouri River region. The other made its way up the Mississippi River. By 1000 A.D. two major Mississippian occupation centers were established. One was located near the junction of the Cannon and Mississippi rivers north of Red Wing, and the other was along the central and upper Minnesota River. Both apparently evolved from the great Middle Mississippian center at Cahokia, Illinois, developing in Minnesota as modified cultures—one adapted to the forests and tall-grass prairies of the east, the other to the timbered river bottoms and grasslands of the west.

Mississippian culture was based on intensive agriculture. The way of life depended heavily upon the cultivation of maize or corn, beans, squash, sunflowers, and tobacco. Timbered areas were cleared in the river bottoms, where small garden plots were planted to these crops.

Above is a hoe made from a bison shoulder blade.

Mississippian chipped-stone tools. (a-d) Triangular projectile points. (e) Drill. (f, g) Hide scrapers. (h) Perforator. (i, j) Knives.

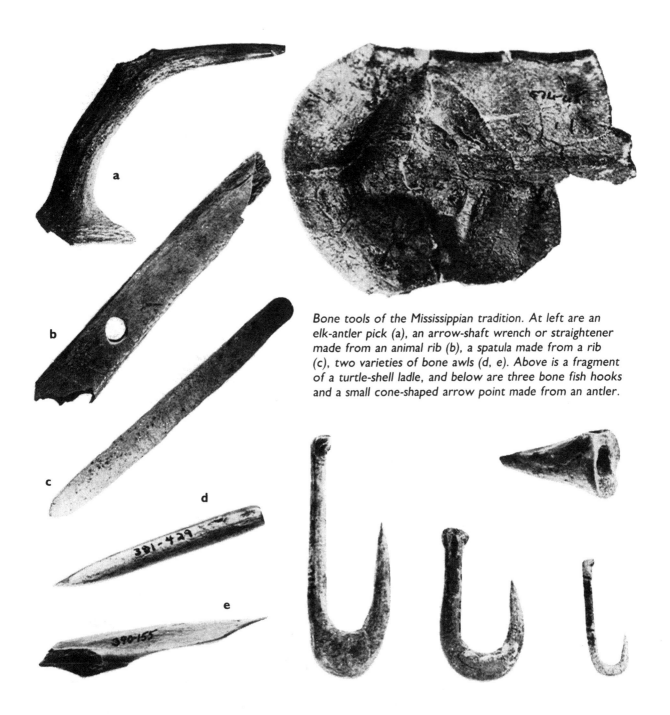

Bone tools of the Mississippian tradition. At left are an elk-antler pick (a), an arrow-shaft wrench or straightener made from an animal rib (b), a spatula made from a rib (c), two varieties of bone awls (d, e). Above is a fragment of a turtle-shell ladle, and below are three bone fish hooks and a small cone-shaped arrow point made from an antler.

Hunting and fishing remained important, however, and Mississippian sites in Minnesota show a dependence upon bison as a staple food.

Villages in this period were comparatively large and may have housed from 600 to 800 people. Sometimes surrounded by a protective wall or palisade, they were frequently located on flat river terraces above the rich bottom lands. Deep underground storage pits for vegetables were dug throughout the villages.

As for tools, chipped-stone technology continued to be important. Well-made arrow points of side-notched and unnotched triangles are very common. Large, double-pointed knives and a distinctive trapezoidal form of hide scraper indicate the continued use of animal hides for clothing. Drills and punches are found as well.

Ground-stone tools included ungrooved axes or celts, small, round, grinding stones, sandstone abraders for smoothing arrow shafts, and a continued use of the stone maul. Pipes of catlinite or

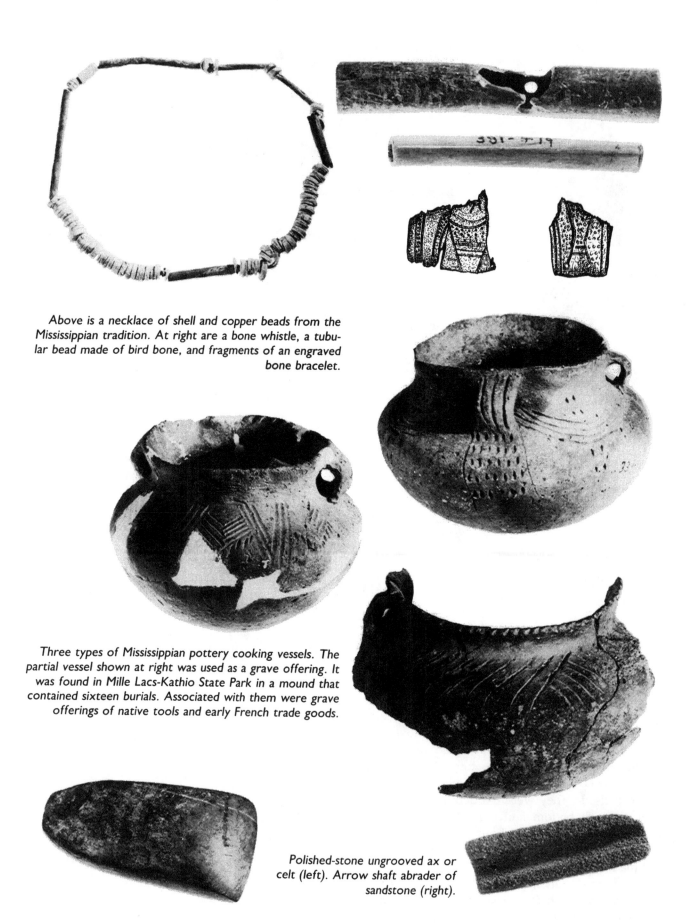

Above is a necklace of shell and copper beads from the Mississippian tradition. At right are a bone whistle, a tubular bead made of bird bone, and fragments of an engraved bone bracelet.

Three types of Mississippian pottery cooking vessels. The partial vessel shown at right was used as a grave offering. It was found in Mille Lacs-Kathio State Park in a mound that contained sixteen burials. Associated with them were grave offerings of native tools and early French trade goods.

Polished-stone ungrooved ax or celt (left). Arrow shaft abrader of sandstone (right).

pipestone from the quarry preserved in the present-day Pipestone National Monument in southwestern Minnesota are very well made.

Bone tools are also plentiful in the Mississippian tradition. A hoe, fashioned of either an elk or a bison shoulder blade, is one of the most frequently found bone tools. Awls, spatulas, fishhooks, dice, and needles of bone are also present. Bone bracelets decorated with engraved designs sometimes occur with burials. Shells are also present, usually as personal ornaments, but sometimes as spoons and dippers.

Mississippian pottery is globular with a rolled or flaring rim, two or four paired handles, and a smooth exterior surface. It is very different in appearance from that of the Woodland tradition. Pottery from the eastern Mississippian sites in the state is tempered with crushed clamshell and decorated with wide or narrow incised geometric designs. That from sites in the Minnesota River Valley is tempered with crushed rock and has both incised and cord-impressed decorations.

Burial mounds continue in this period. Usually they contain primary burials with grave goods. Sometimes single Mississippian intrusive burials turn up in earlier Woodland mounds. Some of the mounds built late in this period in the southern part of the state are distinctive in that the exterior was covered with limestone slabs. Such mounds once existed, for example, at Pipestone National Monument. Burials also occur within villages on occasion, frequently as single primary burials in abandoned storage pits. Cemeteries, too, are found in the southeastern part of the state, where primary burials in shallow, rectangular graves occur along ridgetops or on high river terraces.

Farther north, in the central Minnesota area, an unusual way of life developed which was based on Mississippian patterns but which substituted wild rice for corn as the staple vegetable food. The Cooper Village Site in Mille Lacs-Kathio State Park is an excellent example. Here archaeologists found all the typical Mississippian tools, pottery of both Mississippian and Woodland patterns, but none of the deep food-storage pits characteristic of the corn-growing villages to the south. While the presence of squash seeds indicated some gardening, charred wild rice grains, taken from fire pits and threshing pits in the village, were more common. Nearby burial mounds have primary burials with Mississippian mortuary pottery.

In the northern section of Minnesota, as we have seen, Woodland cultures persisted to the historic period, modified by influences from the Mississippian tradition and dependent to a great extent upon wild rice.

A disc pipe made of red pipestone dating to the Oneota Culture of the Mississippian tradition.

The Past
and the Future

ARCHAEOLOGICAL RESEARCH in Minnesota has changed dramatically since the first nineteenth-century efforts by pioneers in the field. The early contributions of Theodore H. Lewis and his monumental survey and mapping of burial mound groups and of Jacob V. Brower and his efforts to understand the nature of sites and artifact collections at Mille Lacs and in the Mississippi River headwaters have had lasting importance. An invaluable source of information is the book entitled *The Aborigines of Minnesota*, edited by State Geologist Newton H. Winchell and published by the Minnesota Historical Society in 1911, which contains Lewis's mound surveys. Those early archaeological efforts, however, were directed toward questions that differ significantly from those posed by the scientific archaeology of today. North American archaeology was in its infancy in the late nineteenth and early twentieth centuries; it was only in the 1920s and 1930s that scholars devoted to archaeology as a profession entered Upper Midwest institutions and organizations.

In Minnesota, the first intensive work in serious excavation was launched in 1931 by Professor Albert E. Jenks of the University of Minnesota, who had begun his archaeological research in New Mexico and Algeria. He initiated an annual field-research program at the university, and his protégé, Professor Lloyd A. Wilford, continued the program after Jenks retired in 1937. The excavation of historic-period archaeological sites was begun in 1936 with Minnesota Historical Society sponsorship at Grand Portage by Ralph D. Brown and at Fort Ridgely by G. Hubert Smith, a student of Wilford's.

The early efforts of Jenks and Wilford centered on prehistoric sites, and after an initial concentration on possible very early sites following the find at Pelican Lake, Wilford set out to determine the nature of archaeological complexes in the varied environmental settings of the state. He was able to describe the culture content of various prehistoric archaeological units, giving them labels like "Laurel," "Blackduck," "Kathio," "Malmo," "Howard Lake," and others that remain in use today. He was also able to distinguish time sequences for some of the regions of Minnesota, noting the clear stratigraphic separation of Laurel and Blackduck cultures, for example. Because most of his work preceded the development of radiocarbon dating, he was not able to attach precise calendar dates to his sequences.

Archaeologists today are interested in understanding the time and space variations in Minnesota prehistory—how they came about; how societies adapted to different environmental settings; how and why prehistoric cultures changed through time; why there is cultural stability in one region and rapid change in another; what was the size and nature of the social groups in specific archaeological cultures; what foods were present and what was the incidence of nutritional deficiencies. These and numerous other similar questions are posed by archaeologists who shape problems and ask questions in the context of anthropological theory. Their questions are phrased so that archaeological research oriented toward specific goals can provide data to test hypotheses and thus reflect upon the larger theoretical problems. The ultimate goal is to understand human behavior and the change or stability of human cultures. In this sense archaeology is a behavioral science allied with ethnology in the broader discipline of cultural and social anthropology.

The need to increase our knowledge of culture content persists. The cultures of the Paleoindian and Eastern Archaic traditions are poorly known; Malmo and Howard Lake cultures are really represented primarily by pottery or ceramic types and not by the necessary full range of their content; and the number of sites whose archaeological inventories show the presence of the first European trade goods is very small.

Questions of cultural history are numerous and many are unanswered. Cheyenne Indian oral traditions speak about a home somewhere in western Minnesota and an economic system based on farming at a time immediately before the historic period; their stories also tell about the Cheyenne's move westward to the high Plains as nomadic horse-using hunters. But no site in Minnesota that can clearly be identified as prehistoric Cheyenne has been located. Similarly, the Western Dakota or Sioux, who, like the Cheyenne, became Plains bison hunters in the historic period, have Minnesota origins; early French maps locate them on the western prairies near Big Stone and Traverse lakes. Yet sites identified as Late Prehistoric Western Dakota have not been found. These and other similar gaps in the record are important not only to archaeologists but also to native Americans. It is, after all, their cultural heritage that lies buried in archaeological sites, and they have an interest in that prehistoric past.

The archaeology of historic sites has developed rapidly in recent years, and archaeologists have conducted excavations at a variety of sites representing many historic periods. These excavations may be at sites once inhabited by historic native American groups—like the work of Janet Spector of the University of Minnesota in a nineteenth-century Wahpeton Dakota village at Little Rapids near Carver. They may be at French period sites—like the work of Douglas A. Birk of the Institute for Minnesota Archaeology at an early French post near Little Falls—or at English period sites—like the excavations by Alan R. Woolworth of the Minnesota Historical Society at Grand Portage National Monument on Lake Superior. Or they may be at later fur posts, logging and sawmill sites, or military forts. More unusual are the tower foundations and cable anchor sites of Minneapolis's first suspension bridges across the Mississippi, built in 1854 and 1875, recently excavated by Robert Clouse and Jeff Tordoff of the Minnesota Historical Society. Whatever the nature of the historic site, the excavation techniques archaeologists use there are the same as those used at prehistoric sites. While some of the questions posed and the problems raised by historical archaeologists may be different from those of prehistorians, the goal is the same—to understand and interpret the past.

Additional questions about cultural history pervade Minnesota's prehistoric as well as its early historic periods: When did the practice of burial in mounds begin, and what was the source of that idea? Can we trace Siouan-speaking groups back in prehistory to determine the time and direction of their entry into Minnesota? Was the copper used in the Early Archaic cultures obtained only from random pieces of "float" metal in the glacial gravels, or was it actually mined from veins in the basalt rock along the tributaries of the Upper St. Croix River?

There are literally hundreds of similar questions that are potentially answerable through archaeological research. Archaeologists, however, orient their research toward explaining rather than gathering facts of prehistory. While they are interested in the "what," they are much more interested in the "how" and "why." In other words, archaeologists are not only chroniclers of events and change, but they are also students of the processes of human culture that lead us to understand the reasons for cultural change, cultural stability, and specific cultural events.

One example of this approach is the archaeologists' study of the distribution of artifacts and raw materials through prehistoric trade networks. Conclusions about those trade networks help us to understand both the transmission of new elements of culture from an outside area and change within an archaeological region. Another example is the study of settlement patterns that uses data from archaeological sites across a region to locate prehistoric settlements in relation to natural features and the resources available at various seasons of the year. A regionwide approach allows archaeologists to note alterations in the size of the settlements seasonally and through time, related demographic or population changes, and many other factors.

A key element for modern archaeologists is their view of human culture as an adaptive mechanism. According to this view, human behavior and the groups humans live in are modified selectively by several things: more effective utilization of resources; changing tools, weapons, shelters, and other aspects of technology; and the development of labor organization within the group, to cite a few. Studies of these changes are usually based on a comparative analysis of several intensively researched single sites, and they always demand a detailed analysis of the environmental setting and the resources used by the site's inhabitants. C. Thomas Shay's published work entitled *The Itasca Bison Kill Site: An Ecological Analysis* reports the first such Minnesota study and is an excellent example of this view. To understand the site and the activities that occurred there, Shay had to analyze in detail the soils, local geomorphology, pollen grains trapped in the soil, mollusk remnants, animal bone refuse, and plant remains. All of these analyses were done in addition to the usual archaeological studies of the artifacts, the stratigraphy of the site, and the distribution within the site of evidence of human activity. Such comprehensive studies require the cooperation of specialists in the natural sciences who not only perform the analyses but also collect the data they need from the site. Many contemporary archaeologists have acquired special skills in natural science (as Shay did in pollen analysis), but no archaeologist can command all of the knowledge and skills necessary to complete a full report. The research is thus a collaborative effort directed by the archaeologist toward specific goals.

An Oneota pottery vessel in place at the Bryan Site, Goodhue County. Excavated in a salvage project by archaeologists under contract with the Minnesota Department of Transportation. Photo courtesy of the Institute for Minnesota Archaeology.

Minnesota is a superb laboratory for research into human cultural adaptation. It has widely divergent environmental areas offering different resources and even different climates. More important, through time these environmental areas have changed in character and in geographic distribution, sometimes radically. An excellent synthesis of the major vegetation changes of the postglacial era in Minnesota is presented by Herbert E. Wright, Jr., in an article appearing in *Aspects of Upper Great Lakes Anthropology* (published under the editorship of Elden Johnson in 1974 by the Minnesota Historical Society). His work is based on data from a large number of bog- and lake-sediment cores. Because of such thorough pollen studies by paleo-botanists, Minnesota archaeologists have gained a better understanding of their state's past environmental characteristics and change than have their colleagues anywhere in North America.

Another kind of archaeological research has emerged in recent years. It is often called "public archaeology," because it has been stimulated by the federal government's actions that defined archaeological sites as cultural resources important to our national heritage. In 1906 Congress passed a federal Antiquities Act that prohibited the excavation of sites on federal land without a permit. Subsequent legislation provided protection for archaeological sites by allowing their inclusion in the National Register of Historic Places and by establishing State Historic Preservation offices and a federal Advisory Council on Historic Preservation. An Executive Order issued by the president in 1971 requires federal agencies to inventory the "cultural resources" (including archaeological sites) on lands they administer or regulate.

States also have laws governing archaeological activities. Minnesota established a state Antiquities Act in 1939; as modified subsequent-ly, it prohibits archaeological activities on all nonfederal public lands without a permit; it also encourages state agencies and other subdivisions of state government that alter the landscape through construction activities to conduct surveys to determine the possible presence of archaeological or historic sites that may be endangered. Minnesota also has a strict law prohibiting the excavation of human burials—prehistoric or historic—except in unusual circumstances and under extremely rigid guidelines. Such excavations of burials outside of platted cemeteries are directed by the Minnesota state archaeologist and a native American advisory council.

One result of this legislation and regulation has been the addition of trained archaeologists to the staffs of agencies at both the federal and state levels. The Minnesota Department of Transportation contracts with the Minnesota Historical Society for archaeological surveys of highway construction areas, and the U.S. Army Corps of Engineers in each of its districts has employed archaeologists, as has the U.S. Department of Agriculture's Forest Service. The Minnesota Department of Natural Resources has contracted for archaeological surveys of state parks, state forests, and waterways. The State Historic Preservation Office in the Minnesota Historical Society has a staff of prehistoric and historic site archaeologists, architectural historians, and historians who conduct surveys, prepare nominations of sites and structures to the National Register of Historic Places, and assist in determining if an archaeological or historic site survey is needed before any construction is begun on public lands.

An enormous increase in the identification of Minnesota's archaeological site locations has resulted from archaeological surveys recommended under various laws and regulations. The official state archaeological site file, maintained by the state archaeologist headquartered at Hamline University, now contains records of many hundreds of sites.

When archaeological sites are found in areas where they will be threatened by construction activities, the first goal is to preserve the sites by shifting the construction location. Sometimes this cannot be accomplished for economic or other reasons. When that happens, the State Historic Preservation Office will recommend to the federal Advisory Council "mitigation of the adverse impact" of the construction by excavating the site to salvage threatened archaeological data. Several such salvage projects have been completed in Minnesota, adding considerable data to the known archaeological record.

Although the value of the increased information acquired through public archaeology is widely recognized, there is a serious problem in making it available to archaeologists and to the public. Most of the reports carrying the data remain unpublished and unpublicized. This circumstance is extremely serious because the free and open exchange of research results is essential to the health of any science. Questions, problems, and research hypotheses stem from current knowledge, and when that knowledge is not widely shared, archaeological science is crippled.

The success of future archaeological research depends not on archaeologists and their research alone, but on the interest and knowledge of all individuals. How can you further your knowledge and help satisfy your interests? Read the archaeological literature, join archaeological organizations, participate in archaeological activities, visit archaeological sites and interpretive centers, and share your interests

Ancient carvings in red quartzite bedrock can be seen at the Jeffers Petroglyphs Site operated by the Minnesota Historical Society. Photo by Alan
Ominsky, Minnesota Historical Society collections.

and knowledge with others. If you collect archaeological materials from the earth's surface, follow the example of Elaine Redepenning: document your collection carefully and make the results available to archaeologists. Most important, *do not excavate* except as a volunteer or student with a professionally directed field party. Remember that archaeological sites are nonrenewable resources, and once they are disturbed, the vital data they hold are lost forever.

Members of the Minnesota Archaeological Society meet monthly and would be happy to welcome you. Their quarterly publication, the *Minnesota Archaeologist*, is available in many public and all college libraries in Minnesota. You may also join the Institute for Minnesota Archaeology, a nonprofit archaeological research organization, and participate as a volunteer in field excavations and laboratory analyses. Or join the Minnesota Historical Society and read its magazines, *Minnesota History* and *Roots*.

Numerous archaeological sites, interpretive centers, and museums in Minnesota are open to visitors. The Minnesota Historical Society operates the Jeffers Petroglyphs Site in southwestern Minnesota, the Grand Mound Interpretive Center near International Falls, the Fort Ridgely Interpretive Center near Fairfax, the Mille Lacs Indian Museum at Vineland, Historic Fort Snelling and History Center near the Twin Cities, and the museum in its headquarters building near the State Capitol in St. Paul. The Science Museum of Minnesota in St. Paul has an excellent Anthropology Hall and is expanding its interpretation of the state's archaeology. Minnesota has two national monuments operated by the National Park Service, and both are located on archaeological and historic sites. Pipestone National Monument in southwestern Minnesota is on the site of the famous pipestone (catlinite) quarry where historic native Americans over centuries have mined the soft red stone for the manufacture of pipes. Grand Portage National Monument, located on a small bay of Lake Superior at the extreme northeastern tip of Minnesota, is the site of the beginning of the historic portage to the chain of border lakes leading west—a portage begun by prehistoric native Americans, used successively by French, British, and American fur traders, and now traversed by boundary-water canoeists. It is also the site of a major fur post of the early 1800s, a part of which has been reconstructed. State parks at Itasca and Mille Lacs-Kathio offer marked archaeological sites, archaeological collections on display, and summer naturalist programs that feature archaeological interpretations. Many other state and county parks contain burial mounds and village sites that can be visited. There is no shortage of visible prehistoric sites and excavated artifacts in Minnesota, and "seeing" archaeology is a wonderful way to learn.

Enjoy Minnesota archaeology!

Suggested References

GENERAL SURVEYS

American Antiquity, published quarterly by the Society for American Anthropology, is the major professional journal in this field.

Jennings, Jesse D. *Prehistory of North America*. 2nd ed. New York: McGraw-Hill, 1974.

Willey, Gordon R. *An Introduction to American Archaeology*. Vol. 1, North and Middle America. Englewood Cliffs, N.J.: Prentice-Hall, 1966.

STATE AND REGIONAL SURVEYS AND JOURNALS

Green, William, James B. Stoltman, and Alice Kehoe, eds. "Introduction to Wisconsin Archaeology," Special Issue of the *Wisconsin Archeologist*. 67 (September/December, 1986): Nos. 3 and 4.

Johnson, Elden, ed. *Aspects of Upper Great Lakes Anthropology: Papers in Honor of Lloyd A. Wilford*. Minnesota Prehistoric Archaeology Series No. 11. St. Paul: Minnesota Historical Society, 1974.

McKusick, Marshall. *Men of Ancient Iowa*. Ames: Iowa State University Press, 1964.

Midcontinent Journal of Archaeology, published by Kent State University Press, is an excellent regional journal covering the Midwest.

Minnesota Archaeologist, published four times each year by the Minnesota Archaeological Society, has many articles on the prehistory of Minnesota.

Plains Anthropologist, published in Lincoln, Nebr., is a quarterly journal covering the prehistory of an area that includes Minnesota.

Quimby, George I. *Indian Life in the Upper Great Lakes 11,000 B.C. to A.D. 1800*. Chicago: University of Chicago Press, 1960.

Winchell, Newton H., et al., eds. *The Aborigines of Minnesota*. St. Paul: Minnesota Historical Society, 1911.

REPORTS ON MINNESOTA SITES AND CULTURES

Bleed, Peter. *The Archaeology of Petaga Point: The Preceramic Component*. Minnesota Prehistoric Archaeology Series No. 2. St. Paul: Minnesota Historical Society, 1969.

Gibbon, Guy E. *The Sheffield Site: An Oneota Site on the St. Croix River*. Minnesota Prehistoric Archaeology Series No. 10. St. Paul: Minnesota Historical Society, 1973.

Jenks, Albert E. "Minnesota's Browns Valley Man and Associated Burial Artifacts," in American Anthropological Association, *Memoirs No. 49*, Menasha, Wis., 1937.

_____. *Pleistocene Man in Minnesota*. Minneapolis: University of Minnesota Press, 1936. Describes the skeleton find at Pelican Rapids.

Johnson, Elden. *The Arvilla Complex*. Minnesota Prehistoric Archaeology Series No. 9. St. Paul: Minnesota Historical Society, 1973.

Lothson, Gordon A. *The Jeffers Petroglyphs Site: A Survey and Analysis of the Carvings*. Minnesota Prehistoric Archaeology Series No. 12. St. Paul: Minnesota Historical Society, 1976.

Michlovic, Michael G. "The Archaeology of the Canning Site," in *Minnesota Archaeologist*, 45:3–36 (Spring/Summer, 1986).

Shay, C. Thomas. *The Itasca Bison Kill Site: An Ecological Analysis*. Minnesota Prehistoric Archaeology Series No. 6. St. Paul: Minnesota Historical Society, 1971.

Stoltman, James B. *The Laurel Culture in Minnesota*. Minnesota Prehistoric Archaeology Series No. 8. St. Paul: Minnesota Historical Society, 1973.

Streiff, Jan E. *Roster of Excavated Prehistoric Sites in Minnesota to 1972*. Revised ed. Minnesota Prehistoric Archaeology Series No. 7. St. Paul: Minnesota Historical Society, 1972.

Wilford, Lloyd A., "A Revised Classification of the Prehistoric Cultures of Minnesota," in *American Antiquity*, 21:130–142 (October, 1955).

_____. *Burial Mounds of the Red River Headwaters*. Minnesota Prehistoric Archaeology Series No. 5. St. Paul: Minnesota Historical Society, 1970.

Wilford, Lloyd A., Elden Johnson, and Joan Vicinus. *Burial Mounds of Central Minnesota: Excavation Reports*. Minnesota Prehistoric Archaeology Series No. 1. St. Paul: Minnesota Historical Society, 1969.

Printed in the USA
CPSIA information can be obtained
at www.ICGtesting.com
JSHW060049150824
68134JS00031B/2690